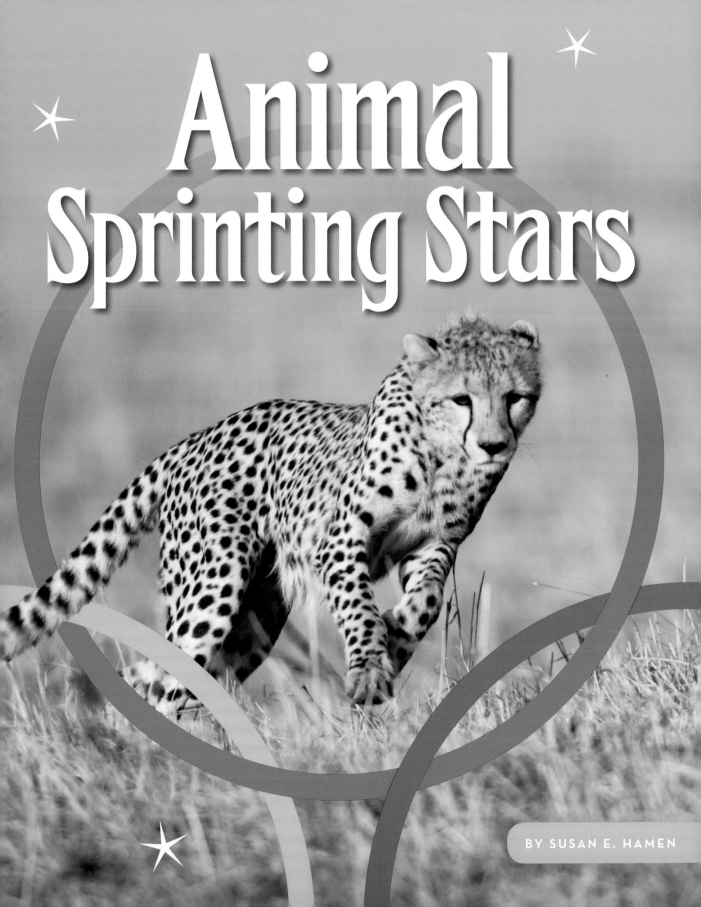

Animal Sprinting Stars

BY SUSAN E. HAMEN

The Child's World®
childsworld.com

Published by The Child's World®
1980 Lookout Drive • Mankato, MN 56003-1705
800-599-READ • www.childsworld.com

Photographs ©: iStockphoto, cover, 1, 13, 20; Stephen Dalton/
Science Source, 5, 10; Frederic Legrand/Shutterstock Images,
6; Shutterstock Images, 7; Matt Jeppson/Shutterstock Images, 9,
21; ZSSD/Minden Pictures/Newscom, 14; Volodymyr Burdiak/
Shutterstock Images, 15; Frank Hildebrand/iStockphoto, 17, 20–21;
Jim Zipp/Science Source, 18

ISBN 9781503820425
LCCN 2016960512

Printed in the United States of America
PA02341

ABOUT THE AUTHOR

Susan E. Hamen has written more than 20 books for children and loves learning about new things when she writes. Her book *Clara Barton: Civil War Hero and American Red Cross Founder* was chosen for the American Library Association's 2011 Amelia Bloomer Project Book List. She lives in Minnesota with her husband, Ryan, and her two children, Maggie and Jack.

Contents

CHAPTER 1

Star Sprinters

Zoooom! The animal world is filled with fast sprinters. Some of these animals are large and powerful. Others are very small.

Humans can also sprint. Sprinting is moving very fast for short periods of time. Many sprinters run as fast as they can in short bursts. Some swim fast sprints. Ice skaters can sprint across the ice on their skates. Sprinters compete in races against other competitors.

Sprinters run short races called dashes. The distance of these dashes is 1,312 feet (400 m) or less. Long ago, ancient Olympic Games had one event. Those athletes ran a short sprint. It was called a stade. Today, sprinters still compete in the Olympics.

Animals sprint to either catch food or avoid being eaten.

Most sprinters wear shoes with spikes on the bottom. These shoes help them run faster.

In the 2016 Summer Olympics, Usain Bolt from Jamaica won three gold medals in sprint competitions. He crossed the 100-meter dash finish line in 9.58 seconds.

This is approximately 28 miles per hour (45 km/h). Cars driving down city streets drive that fast!

Nature has many quick animals. Many run, some swim, and others fly. In this book, three of nature's best sprinters will compete in the Animal Olympics. Which one will win the gold medal?

ATHLETE PROFILE
NAME: Usain Bolt
BORN: August 21, 1986 in Sherwood Content, Jamaica
HEIGHT: 6.5 feet (198 cm)
WEIGHT: 207 pounds (94 kg)
FASTEST SPEED: 27.7 miles per hour (44.6 km/h)
RECORDS: 656 feet (200 m) in 19.19 seconds, 328 feet (100 m) in 9.58 seconds

CHAPTER 2

Water-Walking Lizard

The first athlete is small and green. It lives in the rainforests of Central America. Most animal sprinters only run on land, but not this one. The green basilisk lizard can also run on top of water!

The green basilisk belongs to the iguana family. It eats insects, such as ants, beetles, and grasshoppers. It also likes fish, frogs, and birds. The green basilisk is small. It needs to fight off **predators**, which include larger birds, large reptiles, and snakes.

ANIMAL PROFILE
NAME: Green Basilisk Lizard
LENGTH: 2 feet to 2.5 feet (61 to 76 cm) long, including its tail
WEIGHT: Up to 7 ounces (198 g)
FASTEST SPEED: 5 feet per second (1.5 meters per second)

Basilisk lizards are never far from a body of water.

Green basilisks are also strong swimmers. They can stay underwater for nearly 30 minutes.

The green basilisk spends a lot of time in trees. But it is always close to water. If it senses danger, it drops down into the water.

The green basilisk does not swim to safety like some other animals do. Instead, it stands on its rear legs on the water's surface. Its legs begin to churn quickly, like a windmill. Special skin on the toes of the basilisk spread out on top of the water. As its legs turn, the toes slap the surface of the water. Tiny air pockets are created. These keep the green basilisk from sinking as it sprints across the water. The green basilisk lizard can run on top of the water for approximately 15 feet (4.6 m). The green basilisk then sinks into the water. It swims to safety.

Fun Fact

An adult human would need to run 65 miles per hour (104.6 km/h) to run on top of water like a green basilisk lizard.

CHAPTER 3

The Speedy Cheetah

The next sprinter is the cheetah. The cheetah is the world's fastest land animal. This feline can run up to 75 miles per hour (121 km/h) for short distances. It can gain speed faster than some cars!

The cheetah lives in Africa and small areas of Asia. It roams grassy savanna plains. The savanna is where the cheetah catches most of its **prey**. It hunts gazelles, wildebeest calves, rabbits, birds, and other animals.

ANIMAL PROFILE
NAME: Cheetah
LENGTH: 5.8 feet to 7.1 feet (1.76 m to 2.16 m), including its tail
WEIGHT: 83 to 145 pounds (38 to 66 kg)
FASTEST SPEED: 70 miles per hour (112 km/h)

Cheetahs use their tails to steer.

Cheetahs have special feet that help them grip the ground when running.

Female cheetahs typically hunt alone.

The cheetah sneaks up on its prey. Its coat color and spots **camouflage** the cheetah in tall grasses. When the cheetah is ready, it bursts from its hiding spot. It runs at top speed to chase its prey. It can run up to 45 to 70 miles per hour (72 to 113 km/h). Cheetahs can run this fast for up to 900 feet (92 m). The cheetah uses its paw to trip its prey. The animal it was chasing falls. The cheetah then bites the neck of its prey to kill it. Most hunts last only 20 to 60 seconds.

Fun Fact

A cheetah can reach a speed of 60 miles per hour (97 km/h) in three seconds.

CHAPTER 4

Dive-Bombing Falcon

The last sprinter is the peregrine falcon. This is one of the world's fastest birds. Peregrines live on every continent except Antarctica.

Peregrines hunt other birds in flight. They like wide open spaces. Many live near water and hunt shorebirds. They are also found in deserts. Some even live on ledges of skyscrapers in cities. Peregrines are skilled hunters.

ANIMAL PROFILE
NAME: Peregrine Falcon
LENGTH: 14 to 19 inches (36 to 48 cm)
WINGSPAN: 3.3 feet to 3.6 feet (1 to 1.1 m)
WEIGHT: 19 to 57 ounces (539 to 1,616 g)
FASTEST SPEED: 200 miles per hour (322 km/h)

Peregrine falcons can live for 7 to 15 years.

Peregrines have strong talons that help them hang on to their prey in midair.

But **pollution** killed many peregrines. The species became endangered in the United States in the 1970s. But scientists have since helped the peregrine falcon population increase.

The peregrine falcon flies very high when it hunts. It looks down and can see other birds flying below. It then dives down at its prey. These steep dives can be as fast as 200 miles per hour (322 km/h). The peregrine strikes other birds out of the air. It then feeds upon its prey on the ground. The peregrine attacks songbirds, pigeons, and bats. It will also prey upon larger birds, such as ducks, loons, and geese.

Many peregrine falcons are used to help humans hunt. In a sport called falconry, hunters train falcons to find animals, such as rabbits or small birds. The falcons capture the prey and lead the hunters to it.

CHAPTER 5

The Award Ceremony

SILVER MEDAL
Peregrine Falcon

GOLD MEDAL
Cheetah

Which animal would win in a 100-meter-dash race? The cheetah gets the fastest start and wins the gold medal for first place. The peregrine falcon dives across the finish line for a close second. The green basilisk lizard wins the bronze medal. All three animal athletes have shown their amazing sprinting skills!

BRONZE MEDAL
Green Basilisk Lizard

Glossary

camouflage (KAM-uh-flazh) To camouflage is to hide an animal or person by making them look like the things around them. Cheetahs have spots that camouflage them in savanna grass.

pollution (puh-LOO-shun) Pollution is when harmful chemicals or substances are released into the soil, air, and water. Pollution killed many peregrine falcons.

predators (PRED-uh-ters) Predators are animals that kill and eat other animals for food. Snakes are predators of the green basilisk lizard.

prey (PRAY) Prey is an animal killed and eaten by another animal. Rabbits are prey for hungry cheetahs.

To Learn More

In the Library

Bishop, Nic. *Lizards.* New York, NY: Scholastic, 2010.

Lunis, Natalie. *Peregrine Falcon: Dive! Dive! Dive!* New York, NY: Bearport, 2011.

Marsh, Laura F. *Cheetahs.* Washington, DC: National Geographic, 2011.

On the Web

Visit our Web site for links about animals that sprint: **childsworld.com/links**

Note to Parents, Teachers, and Librarians: We routinely verify our Web links to make sure they are safe and active sites. So encourage your readers to check them out!

Index